Breastfeeding Motherhood

the little breastfeeding handbook

By Gina Michelle

<u>**MEDICAL DISCLAIMER**</u>

The information in this book is not intended or implied to be a substitute for professional medical advice, diagnosis, or treatment.   Always seek the advice of a physician, pediatrician, or other qualified health provider with any medical questions you have.

This book is dedicated to my beautiful Family.

Preface

I remember my mother nursing my two younger brothers when I was a young child. I saw this connection, and the love my mother shared with them. As an adult she encouraged me to breastfeed when it came time. So, before becoming a mother, I knew I would breastfeed my babies.

Gina

Table of Contents

i. Introduction

Why believe *Breast is Best*? Because scientifically-based research includes health benefits from breastfeeding. The medical community promotes breastfeeding worldwide because of these positive results.

A breastfeeding education helps empower new mothers to feel confident in their choice. This book includes information for new mothers and support persons for those planning to breastfeed. Sections include antepartum and the birth plan, transitioning into motherhood, and the postpartum breastfeeding skills such as how often to feed, latch, positions, newborn weight loss, and contraindications. A complete section is dedicated to breastfeeding terms for quick reference in learning the lingo.

Also covered in this text is a brief breastfeeding history, modern social shifts worldwide, scientifically-based research and how it all impacts breastfeeding today.

This book offers a concise yet comprehensive breastfeeding education on many topics for exclusively breastfeeding mothers.

I. Background on Breastfeeding

A. A quick history on infant feeding

Since the beginning of time, mothers would breastfeed their babies after birth because their milk was precious and necessary. Adequate nourishment was vital to survival, especially in the preindustrial era. Most mothers would nurse their own babies, with the exception of few who would pass this duty on to an employed wet nurse. If a mother died during childbirth, a wet nurses could feed a child to prevent starvation of infants.

After industrialization, a surplus of food became available, which helped shift the demand towards alternative milks. In this modern era, breastfeeding became a mundane activity, often seen as old-fashioned, and even perhaps, unattractive. Replacement milks and feeding devices were creatively designed, but often retained bacteria from contamination. Even as late as the 19th century, many babies given an alternative to mother's milk would die. [1]

As technology improved, alternative milks became safer, as packaged baby formulas improved in health and safety. By the mid-20th Century America, formula was no longer the

---

[1] Weinberg F. Infant feeding through the ages. Canadian Family Physician. 1993;39:2016–2020

"rescue milk", but had evolved into the preferred method of feeding for babies. Doctors in this modern era even suggested formula over breastmilk. In 1950, a typical homemade formula consisted mainly of evaporated milk & corn syrup, with suggested feedings 4 hours apart.

Today, baby formulas have improved since the 1950's, offering an iron-fortified and vitamin enriched product. Formula typically comes in 3 different types: Cow's milk protein, Soy protein, or Hydrosylate (a hypoallergenic formula made from a pre-digested cow's milk). These baby formulas are great alternatives to breastmilk, but are not better than a mother's milk. Cow's milk, or as it is coined, *cow's breastmilk,* is technically species-specific to baby cows. A mother's breastmilk is made for her baby.

The cost of formula can be well over $1000 a year, while breastmilk is virtually free. Breastmilk is full of healthy bacteria, live cells, and antibodies made for a human. These cells, antibodies and bacteria actually help colonize the intestines creating a healthy immunity in a newborn. Bacteria in formula is not made for humans, and the goal in formula preparation is sterility.

Breastmilk is the easiest milk for a baby to digest. Digestive issues in a newborn can make things complicated; breastfeeding helps keep things simple.

The composition of human milk is species-specific to human babies, making it superior to any other milk or manmade product for infants. Human Breastmilk contains the most natural nutrition for a human baby, and provides

B. Scientifically-based research supports breastfeeding

Today, a current shift back to breastfeeding is trending. In 1990, the creation of the **Innocenti Declaration** was adopted in Florence, Italy, by **UNICEF** and the **World Health Organization** (WHO). The Innocenti Declaration is a global effort to help improve the health and nutrition of infants by promoting and supporting breastfeeding. The World Health Organization (WHO), along with the American Academy of Pediatrics recommends to *exclusively* breastfeed your baby for 6 months. A recommendation is to continue breastfeeding after 6 months while adding complementary foods until the age of 2. [2,3]

According to the World Health Organization, "Breastfeeding is one of the most effective ways to ensure child health and survival." and

---

[2] Breastfeeding (2018); The World Heath Organization (WHO) Retrieved from http://www.who.int/nutrition/topics/exclusive_breastfeeding/en/

[3] Breastfeeding and the Use of Human Milk (2012) The Academy of Pediatrics

"Breastfeeding protects infants from childhood illnesses." [4] This is because breastmilk is shown to be a unique complex composition made mostly of water, proteins, fats, and carbohydrates, which includes live cells such as leukocytes, pluripotent stem cells, antibodies (immunoglobulins), and microbes which help to colonize and protect an infant's digestive system. [5]

According to the **National Institute of Health,** medical research has shown that breastfeeding provides immune protection, while helping to protect against asthma & gastrointestinal infections. There is also evidence that the longer duration of breastfeeding may provide a greater protection against a childhood cancer (lymphoblastic leukemia). [6]

---

[4] 10 facts on Breastfeeding (2017). The World Health Organization (WHO). Retrieved from http://www.who.int/features/factfiles/breastfeeding/en/

[5] Malgorzata Witkowska-Zimny and Ewa Kaminska-El-Hassan (2017). Cells of human breast milk. Volume 22: 11. Retrieved from http://www.ncbi.nlm.nih.gov/pmc/articles/PMC5508878/

[6] Christine M. Dieterich, BS, MS, RD, Julia P. Felice, BS, Elizabeth O'Sullivan, BA, BS, and Kathleen M. Rasmussen, AB, ScM, ScD, RD (2013); Breastfeeding and Health Outcomes for the Mother-Infant Dyad. Pediatric Clinics of North America, 60(1): 31–4. Retrieved from http://www.ncbi.nlm.nih.gov/pmc/articles/PMC3508512/

According to the NIH, breastfeeding may also assist in earlier feeding cues of satiety, helping to prevent pediatric obesity.

SIDS (sudden infant death syndrome), the unexplained sudden death in infants younger than 1 year of age, remains a partial mystery. But there is evidence that the incidence of SIDS is reduced in babies that are breastfed for at least 2 months, exclusively or even for those breastfed and supplemented with formula. Breastfeeding for 2 months or more is recognized to provide some protection against SIDS. [7]

The composition of a mother's milk provides immunity boosters, but breastfeeding may even give a better workout on the coordination of suck, swallow, and breathe. And there is a theory that breastfeeding helps to build the jaw muscles and hard palate and a stronger airway helping. This

may help an infant to breathe, thus resisting SIDS. [8]

---

[7] John M.D. Thompson, Kawai Tanabe, Rachel Y. Moon, Edwin A. Mitchell, Cliona McGarvey, David Tappin, Peter S. Blair, Fern R. Hauck (2017). Duration of Breastfeeding and Risk of SIDS: An Individual Participant Data Meta-analysis. Official Journal of the Academy of Pediatrics. VOLUME 140 / ISSUE 5. Retrieved from http://pediatrics.aappublications.org/content/early/2017/10/2 6/peds.2017-1324..info

[8] Johnson, Melinda (2014). Breastfeeding Builds a Better Jaw, and Other Benefits for Babies. U.S. News & World Report. Retrieved from

Breastfeeding may help babies bond closely with their mothers in breastfeeding, helping to socialize them from an early age. A study done by the **British Medical Journal** that shows that breastfeeding may even increase the odds toward upward social mobility! [9]

Moms who breastfeed benefit from a quicker recovery from childbirth, a reduced level of stress, and an increased sense of bonding. When a baby nurses from the breast, the mother's body produces prolactin and oxytocin which help moms bond and relax. Breastfeeding also reduces the rate of breast and ovarian cancer. [10]

Today, with research, we recognize that breastfeeding has a whole lot of health and social benefits that just can't be duplicated.

---

http://health.usnews.com/health-news/blogs/eat-run/2014/08/29/breastfeeding-builds-a-better-jaw-and-other-benefits-for-babies

[9] A Sacker, Y Kelly, M Iacovou, N Cable, M Bartley (2013). Breast feeding and intergenerational social mobility: what are the mechanisms? British Medical Journal. Retrieved from
http://adc.bmj.com/content/early/2013/04/24/archdischild-2012-303199

[10] Ages & Stages (2016) Healthychildren.org

Note: Breastfeeding has many benefits for mom and baby, but for those who choose *not* to breastfeed, *can't* breastfeed, or for whatever reason *don't* breastfeed, always support women in their choices. Women should never feel guilty if breastfeeding doesn't work out for them. In our modern world, there are safe alternative options.

C. Modern Shifts in breastfeeding

At the start of the Post-industrial era, the modern trends fell away from breastfeeding. The medical community was suggesting alternate methods of feeding for a newborn. These alternate methods included commercialized packaged formulas and homemade formulas, which were believed to be a better choice than breastmilk. In fact, society began to view breastfeeding with disdain. Today, 70 years later, the modern shift has returned back to breastfeeding because of scientifically-based research.

Today the medical community is likely to promote breastfeeding as the best way to feed a newborn. Note: Promoting an education and awareness on breastfeeding helps encourage a breastfeeding culture.   Promoting breastfeeding does not necessarily mean anti-formula.   Formula is beneficial where breastmilk is not available.

The Baby-Friendly Hospital Initiative

In 1990, the **Innocenti Declaration on the Protection, Promotion and Support of Breastfeeding** (Italy) was produced and adopted by the World Health Organization (WHO) and UNICEF as a global initiative to promote breastfeeding. The goal of the Innocenti Declaration is to promote breastfeeding worldwide for optimal health of mother and baby. This goal is being met through the development of the Baby-Friendly Hospital Initiative.

The Baby-Friendly Hospital Initiative helps hospitals promote a breastfeeding culture, led by an educated staff. This staff practices a breastfeeding policy, educating new mothers on Breastfeeding.

The International Code of Marketing of Breastmilk Substitutes limits promotion of formula in hospitals, also eliminating free samples. The goal is to make breastfeeding the standard. Hospitals that are Baby-Friendly can offer formula only on request and at a cost, or if it's medically necessary. In the case of inability to breastfeed, a wet nurse or milk bank may be considered, especially for preemies.

Note: Formula and pacifiers have historically been promoted as part of afterbirth care. The Baby-Friendly way is to shift from formula and pacifiers, and encourage a natural breastfeeding. In the past, pacifiers were once believed to cause nipple confusion, interfering with breastfeeding. Today pacifiers may be used to provide some therapeutic benefits to infants, and may actually reduce the prevalence of SIDS. [11]

Skin to skin contact
Skin to skin contact is promoted today to encourage a mother, or father, to hold their newborn in skin to skin contact after birth. Skin to skin means holding the baby bare, typically on the mother's chest.

Skin to skin practice helps to comfort a newborn with touch, heartbeat, familiarity of scent, and helps to stabilize a baby's body temperature. Skin to skin contact also helps release oxytocin.
It's a great way to bond with your newborn, promoting familiarity and comfort between a newborn and its parent(s).

The typical image of a mother receiving her newborn 20 years ago included a swaddled baby. Today, with the promotion of skin to skin contact, images are of a bare-bottomed baby lying over a mother's bare chest, with a blanket draped over.

---

[11]Welma Lubbe, Wilma ten Ham-Baloyi, (2017). When is the use of pacifiers justifiable in the baby-friendly hospital initiative context? A clinician's guide. Retrieved from https://www.ncbi.nlm.nih.gov/pmc/articles/PMC5408445/

II. Antepartum (before baby)

A. An Introduction to Breastfeeding:

Welcome to breastfeeding. Learning about breastfeeding before the baby arrives is a great asset.

Breastfeeding is the best way to feed your baby because it is natural and provides the best health benefits for mom and baby. You can be told about how great it is, with backing research, but you won't really understand just how wonderful breastfeeding is until you look down and see a baby staring back up at the mother, while nursing. And you don't need to be the mom to see this.

Breastfeeding provides many things that can't be duplicated. The smell, voice and heartbeat of a mother while breastfeeding helps increase the social bond between mother and baby.

Breastfeeding is more than just feeding a baby. It is about giving the milk that is naturally made, while, providing natural immunity for a newborn. Breastfeeding is about a nurturing relationship which provides security and socialization. Supporting the mother is important to help meet the baby's goals.

Preparation for Breastfeeding
You don't have to physiologically prepare to breastfeed because your body will automatically do this. Before pregnancy, milk duct growth develops during the menstrual cycle. During pregnancy, the milk ducts complete their growth and are ready to deliver milk, or colostrum, by around 6 months. This is all part of pregnancy. Breastmilk production will begin regardless of your choice to feed.

In order to bring milk to the breast after birth, it takes the stimulation of breast suckling to get the milk flowing. This suckling signals the hormones of prolactin & insulin to produce milk, and oxytocin which helps eject the milk. Hormones involved in milk production include estrogen, progesterone, oxytocin, prolactin, insulin, FSH & LH.

Believing you can breastfeed is almost as important as the body's physiological preparation. By mentally choosing to breastfeed, actually helps to make the transition easier.

Plan for Birth
When delivery time is near, you should have prepped a hospital bag, have your list of contacts, and a baby room set up for arrival. If friends or family offer support, make a note of it, don't immediately say no. We often like to deny opportunities that could help us. You may not

need help the first week, but may need help a few weeks in. The early days of new parenthood can be stressful. Supporting the mother is key to supporting the infant.

Planning for what to expect in labor helps prepare for birth. Most new moms-to-be won't know what to expect in delivery, so taking a birthing class will help a mother prepare for labor. The idea of birth often paints an unattractive picture. Labor can be painful and delivery can be difficult, but don't be fooled, the birth of a baby is actually the most beautiful moment in the world. There is beauty in all births.

Creating a Birth Plan helps you collect information, and direct the type of birth you want. Of course, if there are complications, your actual birth may change. But preparing for a natural birth may take some mental preparations. And don't be disappointed if your birth outcome is different than expected, doctors make choices for the healthiest outcome.

A Birth Plan can be written down, or simply discussed with your obstetrician. Keep in mind, hospital policies can have impact on some of your wishes. But you can begin by discussing your medical history, and wishes for delivery. This may define a natural, pain-medicated, or c-section delivery. You may consider an episiotomy, or to heal naturally.

The postpartum (after birth) plan may tell what you want to happen immediately after the birth as well. Do you want your baby immediately placed on you in skin to skin contact? Do you want to hold the baby the first hour, or allow the baby taken away to complete tests? Do you plan to breastfeed? Knowing what to expect is a big part of the birth plan as well.

Plan for After Delivery
Planning for after delivery is as important as planning for birth! We don't always realize this until after we are holding our newborn, wondering what comes next!

What medical tests are done? How do I breastfeed? Where does the baby sleep?

First, the umbilical cord will be cut and clamped at the navel, to separate the baby from the placenta. This separation cuts off all nutrition that was 24/7 via umbilical cord.

A newborn can be placed immediately on the mother's bare chest or abdomen for some skin to skin contact. Then the baby may be moved and wiped clean for some vital checks.

A quick assessment of APGAR is done on the baby the first minute after birth, which includes Activity (muscle tone), Pulse, Grimace (reflex irritability), Appearance (skin color), and Respiration qualities of the baby. This APGAR evaluation is scored 1 minute after birth, and again at 5 minutes. The baby's weight, head and length measurements, and several vital checks will be taken. If the APGAR assessment is low, such as problems with respiration or oxygen, then some interventive care will take place. A gestational assessment, along with a blood glucose test may be done.

After some important checks are complete, and baby's health seems stable, the baby can be placed in uninterrupted skin to skin contact on the mother's abdomen or chest. Placement on the abdomen may also help to expel the placenta from the mother's abdomen naturally. In the meantime the doctor will be making sure the delivery of the placenta is complete, and apply any necessary stitches to the perineum.

Speaking with your doctor before the birth will help reduce surprises.

<u>The Magical Hour</u>
Learning about The Magical Hour before birth is truly incredible. This is a film that features skin to skin contact the first hour after birth.

The Magical Hour film is named and filmed by Kajsa Brimdyr PhD, CLC, who worked closely with international researchers Ann-Marie

Widstrom RN, MTD and Doctor of Medical Science, and Lars Ake Hanson M.D, PhD.

The Magical Hour shows how a newborn, if placed onto the mother's abdomen, in skin to skin contact immediately after birth, will instinctively find its way to the breast to nurse!

There are 9 instinctive stages (as discovered by Ann-Marie Widstrom) [12] that a newborn will go through naturally. These stages begin with the cry, then relaxation, an awakening, a stage of activity, rest, crawling, familiarizing, suckling, and lastly, sleeping. The theory is that if all babies are allowed to enjoy a peaceful hour in skin to skin contact immediately after birth, all babies (without health limitations) will eventually reach the breast to nurse.

<u>When to initiate breastfeeding</u>

[12]

Widström AM, **Ransjö-Arvidson AB**, **Christensson K**, **Matthiesen AS**, **Winberg J**, **Uvnäs-Moberg K**. (1987); Gastric suction in healthy newborn infants. Effects on circulation and developing feeding behavior. NIH. retrieved from http://www.ncbi.nlm.nih.gov/pubmed/3630673

Your opportunity to breastfeed happens soon after birth. The moments after birth are such a special time for the new family. Mom should relax with her new little baby after labor in quiet time. Taking in some quiet time for mom and baby helps both get acquainted.

Once the umbilical cord is cut, the baby starts yearning for nourishment. The baby will recognize the scent exuded by the Montgomery glands. These glands of the breast exude a sebum that has a similar scent to that of the amniotic fluid. This familiar scent will help comfort the newborn and guide him/her to the breast. This is an instinctive bond, which helps reconnect the baby to mom.

Breastfeeding should be initiated approximately one hour after birth, and often, maybe every 1-2 hours for the next 24 hours.

First feedings

This first feeding from the breast will provide the first milk; colostrum. Colostrum is a thick and yellow milk which is rich in antibodies and nutrients. The first feedings are about nutrition and reconnecting the mother with her baby. These early feedings are about making a demand for milk, while providing colostrum for several days.

With continued feedings, the milk comes in between day 3 to 5. This milk is called *transitional* milk. It is creamy and very satisfying to a newborn.

Continued breastfeeding bring in the mature milk, after about day 10. This watery milk may even look a bit gray. Mature milk supplies the growing demand of liquid, and ends with hindmilk, which tends to be a little higher in fat.

<u>Premature Infant</u>
Prematurity in an infant is when a baby is born before full term, which is defined by the World Health Organization as before 37 weeks gestation.

If a baby is born premature, some babies are strong enough to go home, while others may be physically underdeveloped and kept in NICU due to complications.   Breastmilk is beneficial to premature infants because it is easier to digest. Working with the physicians or lactation specialists on methods to provide breastmilk is essential. If the baby isn't able to nurse from the breast, there are other methods of getting breastmilk to a newborn. These methods include pumping from the breast, and then feeding from a cup, bottle, or even a syringe. When the baby becomes strong enough to nurse from the breast this transition can take place.

Expectations of Breastfeeding

The basic 101 of newborns is all about the Feedings! Making sure a newborn receives adequate nourishment is the most important part of new parenting. It is the parent's job to be sure the baby gets the necessary nourishment to thrive.

There are two basic aspects of breastfeeding to understand: the physical and the social. The physical aspect of breastfeeding is the body's ability to produce milk. This ability comes from physiological changes in the mother that helps makes milk available after birth. If a woman's breasts grow during pregnancy, then her body is preparing for milk production. Milk demand produces milk after proper breastfeeding stimulation. There are only a few medical conditions that will keep you from physiologically producing milk. The key is to learning the proper techniques to help develop a good milk supply, and transfer enough milk to the baby through a proper latch.

The social aspect of breastfeeding is the wonderful time spent between a mother and her baby. Because only a mother can breastfeed (with the exception of a wet nurse), only the mother will share this special bond with her baby.

Breastfeeding is a continued relationship between a mother and her baby, after birth. How do you tell your baby you love him/her? The best way is in breastfeeding and sharing close contact with your newborn.

Another social aspect of breastfeeding is in how a mother feels about breastfeeding within a social group. Exposure to attitudes can play a role in how a mother feels about breastfeeding. Finding a social group of peers for support can be helpful.

Becoming a new breastfeeding mother is a transition that can bring stress. Be patient while learning how to breastfeed your newborn. Be confident and secure in your choice to breastfeed. In time, it gets easier.

<u>Successful Breastfeeding</u>
Successful breastfeeding is more than just learning *how* to breastfeed. Successful breastfeeding is to feel satisfied with your overall breastfeeding experience. Whether you only breastfeed for a few weeks, a few months, or even more than a year, the experience will end. When it ends, hopefully you will feel good about the experience.

Learning the proper techniques, exclusively breastfeeding, and learning how to transfer milk adequately is essential to delivering proper nutrition. Knowing to breastfeed 10-12 times a day helps build up a good milk supply and ensures that the baby is receiving enough milk.

<u>Benefits to breastfeeding</u>
The Scientifically-Based Research section expresses some of the medical benefits to breastfeeding. Breastfeeding is promoted by the National Institute of Health, the World Health Organization, and the American Academy of Pediatrics.

Breastmilk helps ensure a child's health and survival by protecting infants from childhood diseases (WHO). Breastmilk is a complex composition made with immunity boosters which help prevent illnesses such as diarrhea and asthma. Human breastmilk is species-specific for human babies offering the proper amount of proteins, fats and carbohydrates, including antibodies, leukocytes and pluripotent stem cells made to protect babies (as cited earlier). The feedings at breast provide not only nourishment, but also may help prevent SIDS.

Breastfeeding has many health benefits while providing an intimate bond between a mother and her baby. This intimacy provides warmth, comfort, and security for a new baby, which helps him/her to thrive.

B. Becoming a new Mom

<u>Believe in yourself!</u>   Think positively toward breastfeeding. New mothers need to believe in their ability to breastfeed. Breastfeeding is so much easier with a support group. New moms can often find breastfeeding supports groups from the hospital they deliver. If this is not available, there are mom groups that may provide support in many areas.
Support can also come your hospital program, or from hiring a Certified Lactation Counselor. This support will help keep breastfeeding feeling normal when others around you do not understand about breastfeeding.

Pregnancy prepares breasts physiologically for breastfeeding. Your body thinks you will be breastfeeding, even if your brain isn't ready! Be proactive; learn the techniques and methods in breastfeeding before the baby arrives. Know that many obstacles can be overcome, and will get easier in time.

A mother breastfeeding is like a symbiotic relationship between the mother and her baby. But instead of it only benefitting the baby (commensalism) it benefits both mother's health and baby's health (mutualism). In addition, the mother typically feels fulfillment in nourishing her baby.

Breastfeeding can become a complex issue if we want to make it one, but it is basically about nourishing your baby. Don't be overly concerned with other people's opinions.

<u>Take Care of yourself</u>
Keep healthy by getting rest, staying hydrated and eating a healthy diet. These are ways to take care of you.   If possible, rest when the baby rests, or utilize help from family or friends so you can catch up when you are run down.

Keeping healthy can also mean to refrain from drugs and alcohol.   Don't rely on stimulants or sedatives which will also pass into your breastmilk.   Drinking caffeine and smoking cigarettes will pass caffeine or nicotine into your breastmilk. It may act as a stimulant giving you a quick energy, but take away later by making a baby agitated or unable to sleep.   Nicotine is linked to SIDS, so never smoke around an infant, and people who handle the baby should always wash their hands after smoking.

<u>Women as caregiver</u>
Women have traditionally become the caregiver because of the division of labor. The family has divided its tasks by gender, with women taking on the child-care duties. Since women carry and produce breastmilk, it seems logical that they've became the main caregiver for children, which encouraged breastfeeding and childrearing.

In the past, women would often nurse one child until the next baby is born.

Postindustrial society invented reliable birth control, allowing women more independence, and consequently having a smaller family size. Postindustrial societies also put women in the work force, which forced men into sharing in some of the child care responsibilities.

<u>Planning & Preparing for a new baby</u>

- Childbirth can be difficult, but you will make it through. Pain control can help
- All women need time to recuperate after the birth
- Caring for a newborn is extremely time consuming
- Your life will change immensely after having a baby

Having a new baby is the most wonderful time in the world, but at the same time it can also be for some, the most overwhelming time! Caring for a new baby is like having a new job. You will need to learn a new set of rules while taking on some extensive responsibilities.

Your life will change after having a baby. Some things will be absolutely to continue after your baby is born, while other things fall by the wayside as your lifestyle changes.

Your new life with baby will become baby-focused, changing your household. Don't lose yourself in having a new baby, find yourself in a family. Get on a schedule, and remember to always make time for yourself and each other in the family.

<u>Work or Stay home</u>

More than half of new mothers are employed outside of the home at least part-time. Becoming a new parent is like adding another job into the mix. Parents often have to balance work into their new parent role. Maternity leave may be used at this time. Each country may offer various amounts of time off for the birth of the baby.

In the U.S., maternity leave for the mother is typically 6 weeks off, unpaid. And fathers typically return to work just days after the birth. Employees can negotiate more time off, especially if an employee is willing to use up vacation and personal days to increase maternity leave.

There is also the option through FMLA which allows mothers and fathers up to 12 weeks time-off un-paid, while securing their positions in leave. However, if the new mother suffers a health issue due to a complicated birth, short-term disability is a possibility.

Each country allows different amounts of maternity leave, some paid, some unpaid. Research shows that in 2018, France, maternity leave is typically 16 weeks paid, and more for a third child. In Canada, maternity leave is typically 17 weeks, sometimes up to a year off paid.

Regardless of what your maternity leave time allowance is, transitioning back to work is a workable challenge. Getting baby on a schedule early will help both mom and baby when work starts.

Being a breastfeeding mother will require mom to get on a pumping schedule. **See Breastmilk storage. You can begin pumping and storing breastmilk for the future use from 3-4 weeks. You can introduce a bottle with breastmilk to the baby at 4 weeks. *Always sanitize all devices used to feed baby for the first 6 months.

Pumping at work is something that should be discussed before returning to work, in order to designate a private area to pump. Pumping breastmilk is a temporary situation requiring accommodation. Pumping breastmilk at work is protected by the **Fair Labor Standards Act**, section 207 ® (U.S.).

This act requires an employer to provide reasonable break time for an employee to express milk for up to one year after the baby's birth.

The French ILO Maternity Protection Convention permits a woman to breastfeed in the workplace. In Canada, Ontario & British Columbia outline rights for breastfeeding in the workplace and in public. Whichever country you live in, look up your laws and negotiate with the employer about a private place to pump during the work day before you return to work.

Simplify Life

Keeping things simple for the first months may help keep things from becoming overwhelming.

Try to plan ahead, helping you mentally prepare for the responsibilities. When the baby is here, just keep moving forward!

Simplify life by removing things of less importance after the baby arrives. Work to focus on developing a new schedule for the baby's needs as well as your needs. Simplifying can be one of the most challenging, but very important ways to transition to caring for a new baby.
Household responsibilities can be kept to a minimum. Washing dishes and doing laundry may be necessary, but spot cleaning floors and the bathroom will suffice for the first month or so. Don't overdo what isn't necessary. The real housework doesn't come until the children get older!

Wear comfortable clothing and throw your hair up, you don't need to look like a superstar! Being a new mom is more about enjoying your time with the new baby!

Entertaining and Social

Having high hopes believing we can entertain for a long evening often ends in exhaustion for the new mom. In reality it can be quite stressful having to tend to guests while caring for a newborn. Be conservative with the invitations for the first month by limiting visits to close friends or family for the first weeks postpartum. This will also limit the amount of germs passed to baby as well. Given the social media world, it's so easy to share images via texts or social media apps.

Ask for Help

Remember, the first weeks of postpartum will be a big transition for mom and baby. It's ok to ask for help from others and express your needs. Try to keep a light schedule and don't take on too much. Having a newborn is a fulltime job. Know that some days will be easy, while others more of a challenge. Hang in there because it will get easier!

Feedings are most important

Feeding your baby will be the most important aspect of parenting, but caring for your baby includes other responsibilities too! You will be changing your baby's diapers almost as frequently as you feed him/her. You will also be changing your baby's clothing, comforting your baby, bathing your baby, and trying to get your baby to nap at the right time. It will all sort of mesh together the first weeks. A new baby is a huge addition and shift of your responsibilities, so hold tight for the ride!

Routine
Organize by *getting into a routine.* A routine helps to establish an order to this new baby stuff. Your routine can be built around the expectations of the day-in-the-life of a baby! An example of a routine can be after the morning feedings to include some seat time while you do the laundry; and some belly time in view while you do the dishes. When nap time arrives, you nap too. You get the basics done while organizing stimulating activities for the baby. Anticipate the needs, and once you get into a routine it is easier on the parent and helps calm the baby in an expected routine. You will be changing a lot of diapers and feeding often, so anticipate that the next time your baby begins to stir, assuming it's probably feeding and changing time again!

Changing diapers before a feeding may be preferable if the baby isn't fussing yet, as it can be more challenging changing the diaper to a sleeping baby. Always change a poopy diaper, even if the baby is sleeping, to prevent diaper rash.

In the beginning, suggested 10-12 feedings happen around the clock. As the baby learns to become more stimulated increasing the daytime feedings, the nighttime feedings may slow down. The amount of milk obtained is the goal, as baby becomes more efficient in nursing, the amount of milk may increase with each feeding while the number of feedings may decline, reducing the nighttime feedings. But some babies will nurse through the night until you wean.

Rest when baby rests
One of the best suggestions is to rest when the baby rests. Getting back on your feet is accelerated with rest. Everybody has different energy levels, but every mother needs to take care of herself after delivering a baby. Keeping daily chores to a minimum, such as dishes and laundry, limiting social visits, while increasing visits of assistance, can help a mother who is caring for a newborn.

Night time Routine
Creating a consistent night time routine helps teach infants about nighttime.
It may help transition the baby into a sleepy mode. Follow a simple routine, being flexible to the baby's needs, but be consistent in the steps and time it begins.

An example of a nice night time routine can include giving the baby a bath at 8pm. After some pampering and getting baby in his/her PJs, you can follow with reading a book in a dimly lit room. Nursing the baby as the evening winds down may help the baby become sleepy. You can use a rocking chair if you wish. When the nursing is complete and the baby is sleepy and ready for bed, be consistent in placing the baby with the back down, into the crib.

But don't be fooled into believing any routine will instantly help a baby sleep for 8 hours! Many newborn and infant babies awaken several times at night to nurse. When a baby cries, you should pick him/her up to nurse. If the baby doesn't want to go to sleep, keep the room dim and quiet during the nighttime, Newborns may sleep 16-17 hours per day, but as an infant becomes more alert, he/she will sleep less. Many infants will have their "days and nights confused".

When the newborn cries at night, it is important to address his/her needs, and assume it is time to nurse. A few rules of thumb include feeding the baby on demand, which will include many night time feedings, and picking up a baby when he/she cries, which will help build security in an infant. As the baby grows older, how you handle your night time routine is up to you, as many specialists will have different opinions.

Creating a nighttime routine will help establish a bed time, and help baby anticipate sleep. As a baby matures and grows, the night time sleeping sessions should increase with age. Teaching the baby the difference between day and night includes keeping the house bright and full of activity, interaction and noise during the daytime hours, and reduced interaction and quiet time in the dimly lit evening hours.

Swaddling a newborn in a receiving blanket is a great way to help baby feel secure, which helps reduce the moro reflex. You can use a blanket swaddle sleeper, and as baby gets older the blanket sleepers help keep the baby warm without loose bedding.

C. Breastfeeding Education before baby

<u>Insight into Breastfeeding</u>
Compare breastfeeding to riding a bicycle. In the beginning you may need support such as training wheels and a coach. But once you learn on your own, you never forget. Breastfeeding is like *riding a bike*!

Breastfeeding may come easy for some, and more challenging for others. Each person is physically unique and each baby is different. Moms who breastfeed more than one child will encounter differences between their babies.

The key is to reach out when help is needed. There will be hurdles, but education and persistence will typically overcome them.

No mother ever feels completely prepared for a baby or breastfeeding. Take comfort in the little successes. Having a support person experienced in breastfeeding and parenting is awesome to help answer questions. If you don't have adequate support, you can always hire a Lactation counselor or a Lactation nurse.

<u>Physiological changes and hormones</u>
A woman's body is awesome. It is awesome on its own, but throughout pregnancy and postpartum it will go through a lot of amazing changes. The breasts develop puberty of a young woman, but they don't complete their full development until after pregnancy.

Here is a brief overview of body changes and hormones during pregnancy:
a woman's hormones (such as estrogen & progesterone) increase vascularization and nutrition for a growing a fetus. Hormones also help in developing the breasts and milk ducts in preparation for milk delivery. Hormones (prolactin & oxytocin) help produce the breastmilk following delivery of the baby.

Although there are many hormones involved, they all play a big part. The woman's uterus and blood vessels grow in size and number due to estrogen, as well as helping the breast tissue to grow and prepare for breastfeeding.

Progesterone helps maintain the placenta during pregnancy and helps grow breast tissue as well. Both estrogen and progesterone are produced from the ovaries and in the placenta.

Prolactin (milk hormone) is a hormone produced from the pituitary. This hormone is kept at low levels but increases during pregnancy. Prolactin is kept in check due to progesterone until after delivery. The progesterone levels decrease once the baby and complete placenta are delivered. Breastfeeding stimulates an increase in prolactin, which in turn produces the milk. If the placenta is retained in the uterus in any way, this can cause bleeding and halt milk production. Communications with your physician group postpartum is important.

Another hormone, oxytocin, also secreted by the pituitary, acts as the milk ejector (when nipple is stretched), allowing the milk to be released from your breasts. This milk release is called the letdown. Oxytocin is dubbed the *love hormone* which may help you feel an emotional bond with your baby. It may help you feel relaxed reducing maternal stress. Oxytocin increases through skin to skin contact. This hormone is responsible for a mother's let-down, sometimes even before the baby begins to nurse!

What is **Lactogenesis**?

Lactogenesis is the production of Milk. There are 3 general stages of Milk production i.e. Galactopoeisis.

- Lactogenesis 1
  the body develops and hormones increase for pre-breastmilk production

- Lactogenesis 2
  the mammary glands shift the hormones into the actual milk production

- Lactogenesis 3
  milk production is mature and established; hormones are leveled out

  Some health issues such as Diabetes or Hypothyroidism may affect your milk supply. Consult with a physician if you plan to breastfeed and have some health or hormone concerns.

Special Time after Birth

The time after birth is very special, and care should be taken to prepare for the first hour. Every mother anticipates holding her brand new baby after delivery, and those first moments after birth are so special. According to the World Health Organization, early and uninterrupted skin to skin contact should take place immediately after birth. This contact can help relax the baby, while bonding with mother, making an easier transition to breastfeeding. It is good to give your baby some time familiarizing herself with this change of environment.

 The skin to skin exposure on mother will be a familiar scent because the Montgomery glands on the nipples emit a similar odor to the placental fluid.

But don't be surprised that most hospitals have a system for tests and procedures for a newborn. If you want uninterrupted time with your baby before you start breastfeeding, you will need to communicate this to your hospital staff.   The traditional hospital process after birth is what happens when the delivery nurse and staff go into autopilot, as mentioned in the Plan for After Delivery. Some steps will be done for records, and some can be done after the first breastfeeding, or while the baby lies on mom's abdomen.

Once the baby is delivered, the umbilical cord will need to be cut and clamped. The baby will be weighed and measured and wiped down. Then the baby is APGAR'd (an evaluation of Appearance, Pulse, Grimace, Activity, and Respiration) at 1 minute after birth to see how he/she's doing out of the womb, and again 5 minutes later. This will help rule out any health issues with the baby. If things check out, the baby can be placed nude onto the mother's nude abdomen for skin to skin contact. The feeling of the warm skin, and smell of the mother, will be very comforting to the newborn.

A Vitamin K shot (essential for blood clotting) will be given to the baby, and an antibiotic ointment will be placed into the newborn's eyes to prevent infection from unknown pathogens from the birth canal. A poke for blood may be taken from the baby's heal to check the baby's blood sugar. These are done for preventive health care and shouldn't delay contact with mom, as they can be done after the first feeding or while baby lies on mom's abdomen.

III. Postpartum

A. Breastfeeding a newborn

The first hour after birth is precious. The bare newborn should be placed onto the mother's bare abdomen or chest in skin to skin contact. This will help familiarize the baby with mother and help lead to successful breastfeeding. Placing a baby on the mother's abdomen or chest begins the first out-of-womb bonding. The baby will actually begin to reach instinctively, and eventually start scooting towards the recognized smell of the Montgomery gland sebum on the mother's nipple (as represented in the Magical Hour). You can help your newborn along and bring the baby to the breast toward the end of this hour of relaxation. It is important that you begin to breastfeed your newborn within the first hour after birth to prevent low blood sugar.

Breastfeeding is a learned activity, for you and baby, so be patient. Offer the breast, helping baby to latch. Most babies will be alert enough to nurse, but babies born under anesthesia or pain meds may take a little longer to be ready to breastfeed.

When you bring the baby to breast, hold the baby in your arms in a comfortable position, with the support of a pillow under the arms (see positions). The baby's belly should face your body, with the arms and legs wrapped around mom.

Tilt the baby's head back a little with the nose near the nipple. Allow the baby's mouth to open wide. The bottom lip should be brought to the breast, allowing an open gape to close around the areola and nipple (the areola is the dark tissue surrounding the nipple) for attachment. When the breast is taken into the baby's mouth, this is the latch. The baby's chin & nose should be touching the breast while breastfeeding. This equal contact to the breast prevents the breast and nipple from being taut.

If the baby has difficulty taking in the nipple and areola in a latch, you can help by lifting and shaping the breast, making it a little easier for the infant to take it in. The lips should not be sucked inwards, lips should be visible with no air pockets around the mouth. The suckle from the newborn will create a gentle tugging to the breast.

The hospital staff will give practical advice and support to help guide new mothers through early breastfeeding. Breastfeeding guidance should include things like latch techniques, and early cues to breastfeeding.

Birth is a bit traumatic for both baby and mother. The baby has transitioned from the womb, to an independent state. The change from constant nutrition in utero, to breastfeeding is a big shift for the infant. Trying to keep up the calories is the goal. For this reason, breastfeeding should closely follow birth, and continue every couple hours in frequency.

The latch will be one of the most important parts of breastfeeding. A proper latch ensures proper transfer of milk. The baby will only take in about a teaspoon of milk the first day. You won't see the amount of milk the baby receives in breastfeeding, but by frequently offering it, you will be providing what is needed. If you want to hand pump a bit of colostrum from your breasts into a clean medicine cup (be sure you wash your hands before you express the milk) you can. If the baby is separated from mom for whatever reason, cup feeding is a great way to give breastmilk nutrition to the new baby.

Be patient in early breastfeeding. The first few days are tiring and trying, but once mom's milk comes in, it will be easy to satisfy the baby. You will know if baby is getting enough by his/her wet lips, weight gain, and satisfaction.

Breastfeeding sessions for a newborn may take time so be patient. A session in breastfeeding may last anywhere from 20-40 minutes. In the beginning they may be short sessions with the baby falling asleep at the breast. But be persistent and nurse frequently to give them time to get what they need. Frequent feedings help demand the volume of breastmilk. Take the time to build up the skills and be patient as baby learns to become more efficient. Feed when in doubt. If it's been 2 hours from the start of the last feed, the next feeding should be due, but you'll probably know this from the baby's cues.

B. Early Breastfeeding Baby Care

<u>Breastfeeding area setup</u>
Setting up an area that will help cater to breastfeeding helps keep things comfy for both mom and baby. Choosing a quiet room, off from the center of the house is a nice escape if the house can be noisy. A seat or rocking chair will hopefully help keep mom upright and awake while nursing. Add a support pillow for breastfeeding and a blanket to help keep the space comfortable when cool. You can keep snacks and water nearby to help mom keep up with her fluids and calories.

You can choose to breastfeed anywhere, but by having a little sanctuary set up for nursing can help with routine and when company stops by.

<u>Positions</u>
Get comfortable and chose your position. Secure your baby in your arms and bring baby to breast. If you are uncomfortable breastfeeding, select a different position. Choose the one that fits you best.

Each position, (with the exception of the football hold) should begin holding the baby's belly toward the mother's belly, with the shoulders and hips in alignment. The arms and legs should wrap around the mother's body for support. You can lift and help shape your breast protruding it a bit for an easier latch. You can use a nursing pillow underneath to prevent arm fatigue while holding the baby.

One way to hold a newborn is in the *Cradle* position. This is the most common position, with one arm supporting the baby's body, while the baby's head is cradled in the elbow area. This keeps the other arm and hand free to make adjustments at the breast.

The baby's belly facing mom's belly with both arms wrapped around mom. The *Cross-Cradle* position uses both arms offering more support than the cradle position. One arm supports the baby's head in the bend of the elbow, and the other supports the baby's body. This position offers the most support and is helpful in a newborn.

If you have large breasts, or the baby is premature, the *Clutch position (football hold)* may be better to bring the baby to the breast. This position allows you to more easily adjust the breast for breastfeeding. The *football hold* will allow you to hold the baby to your side, with the baby attaching beneath the breast. Contact with the breast is ok, but don't let the breast fall onto the baby's face. Be sure there is enough breathing space while he/she nurses!

The *Side-lying* position is where the baby lies sideways, facing the mother who lies sideways, and breastfeeds. The mother's arm may lie behind the baby in support. This side-lying position is good for mothers who are recovering in bed or are very fatigued. Be cautious in sharing a bed with the baby, and stay alert while nursing in this position.

The *Cross-Cradle* hold is great for a newborn. The Football hold is great for a premature baby or for a mother with large breasts. The Cradle hold is great for a baby that is a little older and already experienced in breastfeeding. The Side-lying position is great for mothers recovering from a Cesarean section or who are bed bound.

<u>Baby's cues</u>
Infants are too young to fully communicate their needs. A baby cries for communication. A tired cry is typically continuous, accompanied by eye rubbing or yawning. A cry for hunger is typically a rhythmic, repetitive cry, that builds up and may be accompanied by other cues, such as bringing the fists to the mouth. Don't wait until the baby cries to nurse; crying is too late. Pay attention to early baby's cues for hunger.

Some early baby cues to hunger include awakening, unsettling, which will progress to movement of the fist toward the mouth, smacking of the lips, movements of the tongue and rooting, (the reflex if a baby's cheek is touched, the mouth reaches for it). You will learn to recognize this behavior as demand cues for feeding.

But instead of letting the baby get upset, anticipate the baby's hunger with the earliest cues, and by watching the clock. This anticipation will result in easier feeds and a more satisfied baby, which makes parenting more satisfying.

The Healthy Children's Center for Breastfeeding suggests nursing every 1-2 hours, or *at least* every 3 hours in the daytime, and *at least* every 4 hours at nighttime (even if you need to wake the baby). You should offer the breast between 10-12 times every 24 hours for a newborn baby. This will ensure the opportunity for milk to satisfy the baby. An early hunger cue for an infant can be simply waking up!

When the newborn becomes alert from a sleep, and it's been 2 hours, it is time to nurse. If the baby begins to get uncomfortable, assume it is time to nurse. When in doubt, nurse! As the baby grows older, you will know when it's time to feed. When you respond to your baby's cues, this is feeding on demand.

Waiting until your baby cries is too late. If you wait too long, it can make the latch difficult. Always try to keep the baby calm before breastfeeding. Always prepare for a potential feeding, especially if you will be away from home.

<u>Proper Latch</u>
Breastfeeding is a complex system of jaw movements incorporating a suck and swallow pattern. All parts need to work properly in order to transfer milk from the breast to the baby's belly. The latch is how the baby's mouth attaches to the breast. You want the latch to create a seal, which allows the suction to withdraw milk from the breast. A proper latch may take time especially with a newborn, when the suction isn't yet strong.

A good seal is when the dry lip vermilion is on the outside of the breast, while the wet inner side wraps around the breast, creating a wet seal. If the baby is drawing milk from the breast, you will see wetness around the seal if they're getting milk. If the lip is drawn inward, gently pull the lip outward. If you hear a whistling sound, inspect the baby's mouth. If air is escaping then there isn't a proper seal.

Breastfeeding shouldn't be painful. Check for a proper baby position and proper latch if there is pain. A poor position can over-tug on the nipple. An improper latch can lead to improper sucking. Both can result in painful or bleeding nipples. The jaw movement should be like a rocker motion, it should not be only up and down. The cheeks shouldn't be straining or sucked in too much; the movement should flow.

Once there seems to be a proper seal, listen for the sucks to swallow ratio. In the beginning, before the milk is established, the suck to swallow ratio may be 5 sucks to one swallow (5:1). But once the milk comes in, there should be only 1 to 2 sucks for every swallow (1:1 or 2:1). If the baby has adequately transferred and swallowed adequate milk, there will be satisfaction on the baby's face, with the baby's arms dropping off to the side in relaxation. This relaxation after an infant feed is considered satiety.

<u>First days of milk</u>
The first milk is called Colostrum. It is the pre-milk which is very concentrated and nutritious. Colostrum contains antibodies from the mother.

Colostrum is produced for the first few days before the transitional milk comes in. Although colostrum is in small quantities, it is dense nutrition and very important to providing immunity and antibodies.

The rule is Supply & Demand; the more demand (suckling) from the breast, the more supply (milk) will be produced. In the beginning, newborns nurse inefficiently which keeps the baby at the breast longer. This time increases stimulation which helps produce more milk. The wait for the milk supply can be a struggle, but be patient. Frequent breastfeeding will be rewarded with a good milk supply.

You don't need to see the milk to know whether baby is getting enough milk (after it comes in). If you feel the milk letdown while you are nursing, it seems your body is producing milk. Listen to the baby's swallows. If the ratio of sucks to swallows is 2:1 or 1:1, it seems the baby is properly transferring milk. If the infant seems to have satiety after a feed, this indicates the baby is content after nursing.

After a baby is born, there should be some *well child care visits* with *weight checks.* Medical professionals recommend follow-up with pediatricians for the first weeks after hospital discharge.

This is especially important for breastfeeding babies to help in monitoring adequate weight gain. These appointments evaluate the baby, the baby's weight and rule out issues with absorption or issues with thriving.

Growth Spurts

Growth spurts will put a greater demand on milk with feedings often "clustered" closer together in the evening. Think of it as stocking up before bedtime! Don't think that if the baby wants to continuously nurse that you aren't producing milk. Remember, adequate milk transfer is determined by evaluating the infant's satiety after the feed. If the baby keeps wanting to nurse, but seems relatively content otherwise, it is likely a growth spurt. However, if the baby doesn't seem happy after a feed, keep them at the breast longer. This will help build your milk supply to match the demand.

Growth spurt ages are unique to each baby, but here are some average ages: 8-10 days, 3-6 weeks, and 4-6 months.

Oxytocin, Letdown & Contractions

In breastfeeding, there is a relationship between hormones and milk release. When a baby suckles from the breast, the pituitary releases a hormone called Oxytocin. Oxytocin causes an involuntary reflex which releases milk, allowing it to flow into the breasts. This flow to the breast is called the letdown.

Nursing triggers oxytocin to be released. This hormone is the milk ejector hormone, but it also contracts the uterus after delivery, helping it to return to the pre-pregnancy size. This can cause some pain for the first 2 weeks after delivery, but will go away. Oxytocin can make you feel relaxed, and even sleepy while nursing. It is also dubbed the "love" hormone possibly helping you to bond and love your new little bundle of joy!

Letdown is typically triggered by nursing, but after a while the letdown can be triggered by other things associated with the baby, such as a baby's cry. If you aren't nursing and you have the letdown, your breasts will likely start leaking.

In the beginning, letdown can be a warm, heavy feeling, which can cause a bit of discomfort. Breasts can be very full, even a bit engorged in the beginning, making it uncomfortable. If you are nursing and the baby is having difficulty latching, it may be because the breast is too full and the nipple isn't soft.

This engorgement may be because you aren't nursing frequently enough. If the breasts are too full for latch, try expressing off a little milk to help soften the latch. You can express with a manual pump or hand express.

<u>How often to breastfeed</u>
How often to breastfeed is one of the biggest questions, and unfortunately the answers are variable. Today we recognize that breastfeeding your newborn frequently is so important to ensure the baby gets enough nutrition. Some sessions of early breastfeeding can transfer smaller amounts of milk than desired, so it is important to offer nutrition frequently. The recommendation is to breastfeed your baby at least 10-12 times a day to help ensure that the baby gets enough calories. This frequent nursing is

also important to stimulate the breasts which will help provide a supply to the demand.   The stimulation of suckling will increase the prolactin and oxytocin, which helps to increase the milk supply.

The mother should mentally prepare to nurse. With a newborn, you need to frequently nurse, approximately every 1 ½ - 2 hours.   Each newborn will have his own way of trying to communicate his need for milk, so anticipation is key. Recognizing feeding cues, may include lip-smacking, rooting, and sucking on his fist. In fact these clues can actually be a late sign of hunger.

If the baby is already crying, this stage is too late, and can make latching difficult.

You should instead automatically initiate to nurse a newborn, and when the communication for nurse demand is learned, you learn to feed on demand. When the baby's needs are satisfied and the baby is content, this can be the most rewarding part of early parenting.

<u>Milk production</u>
If your breasts grew larger during pregnancy (Lactogenesis I), this is a sign that the breasts have developed in preparation for milk production. When the baby suckles at the breast, prolactin and oxytocin is released, helping to bring the milk to the breast for the baby to drink (Lactogenesis II).

Within an hour of birth you should begin to nurse. Colostrum, a concentrated first milk postpartum, is produced from the breasts after birth. The consistent nursing puts a demand on the body for mature milk. The Colostrum or early milk is in smaller quantity, but it is there until the mature milk comes in. The mature milk, which is much more watery than colostrum, comes in between day 3-5 on average. Keep nursing with colostrum until the milk comes in, and keep nursing after the milk comes in!

When the milk comes in you will know because your breasts will be heavier and you will hear the swallows. There will be a faster flow of milk and some babies have trouble keeping up and may cough from swallowing too fast. You can gently pop them off if they have trouble, and reattach when they are ready.

You will hear the repetitive swallows when the milk flows until baby's satiation. The heaviness of the breasts should lighten up as milk has been transferred to the baby. You may see milk on the nipple when the baby pops off, and the opposite breast may begin leaking while nursing.
When an infant is actively nursing his/her body may seem tense. When the baby finishes a nursing and is satisfied, he/she will typically become very relaxed, releasing the nipple with the baby's arms falling to the side. The baby often falls asleep in satiety.

The way to increase your milk supply is to nurse frequently and consistently. By keeping the baby at the breast longer, this stimulation sends a message to produce more milk. Don't expect quick feedings in the beginning, efficiency isn't typical for newborns.

As mentioned earlier, a good ratio of sucks to swallows is 2:1 or 1:1. This will tell you if your baby is getting enough milk once it comes in.
 Again, you may see the wetness of milk on the baby's lips, both a good indicator of a good

supply of milk. The baby's sign of satiety is the true test of satisfaction.

Feeding on Demand

In the beginning you should nurse whenever it seems the baby begins to stir. The cues are subtle in a newborn, as initiation of feedings is recommended.

Although it is recommended to nurse 10-12 times a day for the first months, you will begin to learn the baby's cues.   As the baby gets older, the mother is usually in tune with the baby's needs, as cues are much more apparent. Some babies feed more often, or longer than other babies. Feeding on Demand is the idea that the mother nurses when the baby wants to nurse.
When you tend to your baby's needs, the baby gains a sense of security and satisfaction. The baby recognizes this communication is acknowledged, and is rewarded with the needs of nutrition and comfort. Nursing is more than simply feeding, it is about building a relationship, and this is so important for the first few months.

If you wait to feed the baby or skip a feeding, this will frustrate the baby and have a negative impact on your breastmilk supply. Staying on top of necessary feedings keep the baby happy and your milk supply in production. The baby will go through times when she requires more frequent feedings and nutrition, such as in illness or growth spurts, so please adapt to your baby's demands. Breastfeeding supply usually becomes consistent by about 2 months into breastfeeding.

Breastfeed: One breast or Two?

In breastfeeding, you need to equally build up your milk supply, as you need to equally empty each breast. You will do this by frequently nursing from both sides, alternating.

Do you need to nurse from both breasts? Yes, but not necessarily in the same feed. Nurse from one side and when that empties, nurse from the other if the baby is still hungry. You can start the next feeding from the side that wasn't emptied or the side that is fullest, usually the same. Some babies will be satisfied feeding from only one breast at a time, and that is fine.

It isn't always apparent which breast needs to be emptied first to keep it equal, if you have difficulty remembering which side to nurse next, you can place an extra breast pad into that side of the bra as a reminder.

Monitoring diapers

You will be asked to monitor the number of poopy and wet diapers a baby produces after he/she goes home. This monitoring indicates adequate nutrition and absorption. The number of wet and

poopy diapers ensure that milk is being produced and passed through baby, indicating digestion and absorption. Stool color and
odor can be an indicator of malabsorption. Diaper monitoring is a tool used to make sure everything is ok. It's best to refer back to your pediatrician for the number of wet & poopy diapers they want to see per day.

The general rule of thumb for wet diapers is to expect 1 wet diaper on day one, and at least 2 on day two. The colostrum usually transitions to milk by day 3, steadily increasing the expected wet diapers of 3-5.   By day 6 you should see 6-8 wet diapers per day. After the first week, the baby should produce at least 8-10 wet diapers per day.

Wet diapers means there will be wetness on a diaper, which may only be a tablespoon! If the highly absorbent diaper doesn't show wetness, the absorbent filling will change shape a bit. Wetness indicates there is milk flowing through the baby's digestive system.

The poopy diapers rule of thumb is to add one diaper per day for the first few days. Day 1 has 1 poopy, day 2 has 2 poopy. The first poops will be very dark green, almost black, which is due to meconium. This meconium clears out after a few days and is replaced by regular stools. As the breastmilk supply comes in around day 10, the poopy diapers will likely be around 3-5 per day.

The color of poopy diapers (if exclusively breastfed) will become yellow and seedy (like little curds). They may smell a little acidic, but if the color is off, or they are very stinky, bring it up to the physician. The breastfed poops can be a little runny, but is easy to pass for the baby. Always change a poopy diaper to prevent diaper rash.

If you supplement with formula, it will change the consistency and smell of your baby's stool, often significantly reducing the number of stools per day. Breastfed stool is easy to clean and smells a little better than formula stools.

Newborn weight loss
The monitoring of weight loss and weight gain is essential for the first weeks of life. The weight loss with the weight gain can indicate breast milk production and absorption and thriving of the baby.

The first weight on record will be the birth weight. There will be a weight record on about day 3, when the baby is released from the hospital. After a baby is born, there will be some weight loss because the newborn no longer has a placenta to nourish it 24 hours a day. The original replacement nutrition is the first milk; colostrum. Colostrum is dense in nutrition & filled with antibodies, but doesn't provide much fluid. This lack of fluid creates a weight loss. The best way to avert too much weight loss is to frequently breastfeed, bringing the colostrum to the baby, and placing a demand for breastmilk.

Over the next 10 days, the goal is to get the baby's weight back up, surpassing the birth weight. The well child care visits are often set to evaluate if the baby is receiving and absorbing adequate nutrition, which indicates that the baby is thriving. The rule of thumb is for baby to not lose more than 7-10% of the birth weight. If the baby's weight falls below 7%, there will likely be suggestions to supplement with formula.

Mother's milk should be in by about day 3 to 5, which should start the weight gain up past the birth weight, and beyond. If the baby's weight is not gaining, the questions to answer is if there is an adequate milk supply, if there is enough frequency of feedings, or if there is an absorption issue. Too much weight loss can result in dehydration and death of the infant.

There are some health issues that can result in a true low milk supply. The postpartum mom may have an underlying hormonal issue which has gone undiscovered, such as hypothyroidism. Close watch on the newborn's weight is the indicator of whether milk is being produced.

There are a few factors that would naturally decrease a mother's milk supply including pseudoephedrine products, birth control, and nicotine.   These medications should be eliminated, or discussed with the physician who oversees the infant's health in breastfeeding.

Pediatrician visit –Well Child Care Visits
If you are breastfeeding, you will likely need to visit your child's pediatrician several times during the first few weeks of life to be sure the baby is thriving.   These visits will check the general health of your baby, while closely monitoring weight gain of the infant.

This initial visit after hospital release evaluates the baby's overall health and weight check. This weight check is calculated with the birth weight to evaluate newborn weight loss and weight gain. The number count of the wet & poopy diapers will help confirm nutrient absorption. Any issues of digestion (diarrhea, vomiting) should absolutely be discussed at this time.

Proper absorption and weight gain ensures thriving in an infant, which is mandatory for baby's survival.   The communications between the infant's caregiver and the physician is a relationship to oversee the health of the newborn, and to discover any issues early on. Keep these early visits because they are very important, especially if you are breastfeeding.

Dehydration –Loss of Fluids
Always contact a doctor if your baby is vomiting, has diarrhea, and is having loss of fluids. If the

skin or eyes are yellow, and the baby seems irrationally irritable, contact the baby's pediatrician.   Illness and digestive issues can manifest in diarrhea and vomiting, causing dehydration. Dehydration is a serious concern in newborns and can cause death. When in doubt, call the pediatrician.

Diet and breastfeeding

Before delivery you probably haven't thought much about the diet you will eat while breastfeeding. Now that you are breastfeeding, enjoy a well-balanced, varied diet including proteins, fats, & carbohydrates.   Try to eat healthy, getting enough proteins, but don't diet to lose weight by cutting out fats or carbs. You will need these for breastmilk.

Eating a bland diet in the beginning may help things run more smoothly. Drink lots of water and beverages, but try to exclude alcohol and caffeine.

Food Allergy or Sensitivity?

Eat what you want, until you are faced with an irritable baby, and have ruled out other explanations.   If baby is producing foul-smelling stools, has slow weight gain, or has skin reaction such as hives, this could be an allergy or absorption issue.   If baby is vomiting after a nursing, this can be a medical condition such as GERD. These concerns must be discussed with your pediatrician or a physician.

Sensitivities are not allergies or disease. Occasionally what mom eats may cause sensitivities and temporary distress in a baby, such as gas. This seems to become common at about 2 months. Consistent burping of the baby may help relieve the gas. Gas drops (simethicone) will help the baby pass the gas. But if your baby's distress can be associated to something you ingest, such as grapefruit juice, then why wouldn't you remove it from your diet?

You can keep a mental note or a paper journal to jot down the foods you eat, to see if there is a correlation to the baby's fussiness. If you notice the suspected culprit, which can be hours later, remove it from your diet. You can always reintroduce it again later. Babies can also outgrow sensitivities.

Even though any food may cause a sensitivity or distress in babies when passed through breastmilk, a list of common foods can include, broccoli, citrus, dairy, cabbage, garlic, spices, chocolate and coffee. Each baby is unique, so don't assume if your first child is sensitive to dairy, that your second child will be sensitive to dairy as well. In sensitivities, you don't have to eliminate the item from your diet if it is not a true allergy, but it makes sense to eliminate an item that causes some type of distress in your baby. Keep in mind, not all distress symptoms will be diet related.

<u>Baby Blues</u>
The Baby Blues may be seen as mood swings after a birth of a child. It is important to understand that a woman's hormones will shift after delivery.

Physiologically, a pregnant woman has high levels of estrogen & progesterone while pregnant, and after delivery these levels drop significantly. This drop in hormones will often cause a weepy, sad effect in a new mother, just a few days after delivery. This is normal and called Baby Blues. It should pass without much despair.
The general time that this low feeling from hormones should normalize is within about 2 weeks postpartum. Some theorize that breastfeeding may help to normalize the hormones.

Having a baby and recovering from childbirth can be a stressful time for mom. Adjusting to and caring for a new baby is challenging. If a mother is struggling, she needs help and support. Support needs to help her get rest, and help her with the responsibilities to help in caring for the baby.

But feelings of sadness are different from needing help. If mom is having a difficult time with sadness, which affects her ability to care for her baby, or has feelings of wanting to hurt herself, or the baby, it is so important to REACH OUT for help. A depression that continues or turns into a psychosis needs immediate intervention.

If you are a mom who is struggling, please reach out for help. If you are a support person for a new mom who is struggling, please find help. Reaching out for help can be to contact the mom's primary care doctor, or a mental health professional, or even the hospital where the baby was delivered. A referral of specialty should be given.

The National Suicide Prevention Lifeline at 1-800-273-TALK (1-800-273-8255) .

Breastmilk Storage, Pumping & Stocking Up
At around 3-4 weeks postpartum, while exclusively breastfeeding, you can begin pumping and storing extra breastmilk for future use. Continue to breastfeed your baby for each meal, but start pumping off extra milk after a feed. Pumping 20 minutes after the first breastfeeding in the morning, or after the last meal of the night doesn't affect the supply for the infant. You can use a manual or electric pump, or even hand express. Always pump breastmilk with sterilized pumps and bottles to prevent contamination. You will probably only pump off about 1-2 oz. of milk at each pumping.

If you want to combine breastmilk from different pumpings, you can store the first 2oz. in the fridge, and top it off with another cooled 2oz. of breastmilk. This milk from the bottle can then be transferred to breastmilk storage bags with labels. In the beginning, it is easiest to store breastmilk in breastmilk storage bags of 2oz. or 4oz. These bags should be labeled with the date.

According to the CDC, breastmilk stored in a freezer with a temperature of 0* or below is ideally to be used within 6 months, but up to 12 months is acceptable. This seems best in a deep freezer with consistent temperatures. Many others recommend storage in an upright freezer limited to about 3-4 months because of inconsistent temperatures.

As you slowly increase your milk supply, you can pump off about 2 bottles a day if dedicated. The milk supply is slowly increased with extra milk pumping, while trying to keep up with the baby's current demands. If you stop the extra pumpings, or if the baby reduces feedings due to illness, the milk supply will slowly go down. Always use the available milk *first* for the baby's breastfeeding needs.

<u>Return to Work</u>
If you will be pumping several feedings while away from your baby, try to pump milk for *replacement* bottles as needed for the baby's meals. Breastfeed your baby before you leave for work, and after you get home. If the

baby nurses at 10am, 12:30pm, and 3pm at home while you are at work, you would want to pump near these same times. It may be best to use a professional double pump, one recommended by medical professionals. This will be the most efficient way to withdraw the optimum amount of breast milk.

This example schedule would be to pump every 2-3 hours at work because the infant feeds this often (more often for a younger infant). By pumping from both breasts, it may yield more breastmilk. This will help keep up the supply with any missed replacement feedings. Continuing to breastfeed at home is essential to keep the milk supply up.

Note:
Never reuse a bottle that isn't finished. Never refreeze human breastmilk after it has been thawed. Use it up, or toss it.

Co-Sleeping
Co-Sleeping can be dangerous. Staying near your baby is wonderful, but keeping the baby safe is more important, especially when they are newborns. The idea of co-sleeping with your baby during breastfeeding may seem natural for a fatigued mother. In fact, many cultures outside of the U.S. sleep with their babies. But sleeping with your baby may cause a dangerous situation, and risk suffocation. The American Academy of Pediatrics warns against bed sharing. If the baby

sleeps with another person, this may restrict the space for the baby.

Newborns are vulnerable because they are so delicate and should never co-sleep with others. Newborns should have a safe and separate bed from their parents and siblings. A sleeping parent is unable to attend to an infant who rolls over onto soft bedding, or slips under blankets . Parents in deep sleep can occasionally roll onto a baby as well. And never, in any circumstance, should you bring a child into your bed if you are on sedation medications or alcohol.

If you want to keep the baby near, use a bassinet in the room, or perhaps a co-sleeper that butts up to the bed for the first weeks.   But get into the routine of placing the newborn into a separate bed after a feeding.

You should choose a feeding seat, such as a rocking chair to keep you upright while you feed. After the feeding, place the child back into their bed.

Establishing sleep areas
Because it is best to place your baby down for separate sleeping areas, building a routine is essential. Placing the baby down for the night is good for establishing a separate sleeping area. Sharing a room with a bed such as a basinet is nice, but the baby will outgrow this bed. For this

reason, it is good to move them eventually to their own bed in their bedroom. This helps establish a separate sleeping area, where the baby isn't dependent on your sounds. This also gives the parents some private time.

Establishing the night time comes from the routine after the "last" nursing. Dim the lights, and quiet the house. Once the baby completes this nighttime routine (bath, snuggle, nursing), you can gently place the baby into their crib. Make this a comfortable time for the baby, helping to ease them into rest.

Establishing safe sleep areas is recommended by The American Academy of Pediatrics by eliminating soft surfaces for the baby's sleep. This includes crib bumpers, comforters, pillows and stuffed animals. Even a pillow-top mattress or a sofa can create an air pocket, limiting fresh air if the baby rolls into a position of which he/she can't get out of, which could possibly lead to suffocation.

When placing a baby down for bed, place them down on their back, on a firm mattress with tight fitting sheets. The baby's bed should have tightly fitted sheets over the mattress, no bumper pads and no loose blankets to prevent loose bedding hazards with young babies. Infants can be put in a blanket sleep sack instead of under blankets.

The cribs, along with car seats, and any infant seat should be checked for updated safety regulations and recalls.

Breastfeeding and sexuality
Breastfeeding is not sexual. The function of breasts in lactation should not be confused with the sexual function. Intimacy will be a part of breastfeeding between you and your infant, but it should in no way be viewed as a sexual act. Nobody thinks of delivering a baby as a sexual act.

Do breasts become off limits to your sexual partner while you are lactating? This is a personal question, but may be a question for new breastfeeding mothers. There can easily be a separation of sexual activity and breastfeeding with 2 rules: keep the milk for the baby, and clean the breast before baby feeds.

Rest
Leaving the hospital for mom is like recovering from a surgery, while at the same time being handed over a newborn. Support for mom in the first weeks is very important. Recovery is essential in order to handle one of the toughest jobs -caring for a newborn around the clock!

Simplify your life by removing things of less importance after the baby arrives (see the Simplify section). Maintain the household by doing the minimum of amount of chores.

Reduce your previous responsibilities and allow yourself to have down time with your baby. You'll never get this time back.

One of toughest parts of parenthood is dealing with the fatigue. If you are tired, getting adequate rest is the best way to gain strength. But when does a new mother rest? ***Rest When the Baby Rests***, with the baby in a safe sleep environment. Newborns will sleep on average 16-17 hours a day. You can justify napping in the daytime because you are up at night.

<u>Reducing Stress & Increasing Support</u>
Moms often feel stressed because the new baby needs her so much. After the baby's needs are met, mom's needs should be met. It is challenging to know someone needs you 24/7! It feels like the baby is tied to you sometimes. This is why moms should get a break, and occasionally escape! Breastfeeding moms sometimes just want to hand the baby over to someone else for a change. And they shouldn't feel guilty.

Having a support person to give mom a break is a great asset. This can also give the support person some wanted baby time! Having a caregiver come in to help with the chores, or take the baby for an hour or two can help prevent that overwhelming feeling.

A support person can rescue mom by caring for the infant while mom steps out, or simply retreats to a separate area of the house. A support person also helps socialize the baby with others. Pumping and storing breastmilk down the road can give mom more time out for an afternoon, or an evening.

Illness
If a mother is ill, it is still safe to nurse your baby. If you practice good handwashing techniques you may not spread the illness. A breastfeeding mother is already producing some antibodies to her illness in her breastmilk. An ill mother should keep up on fluids, and should consult if taking any medications while breastfeeding.

If mom is vomiting, or has diarrhea, practice extra special preventive measures of hand-washing to prevent transferring the illness to the baby. Keep up on fluids and seek help in caring for the baby.

When the baby is ill, it is always best to continue to breastfeed to provide needed nourishment and comfort. An increased desire to nurse can also indicate illness.   If the baby has signs of fever, vomiting or diarrhea in an infant, contact the baby's pediatrician for risk of dehydration.

Breastfeeding in Public
Breastfeeding has been in the spotlight due to social media posts or even in commercials promoting it. Some see this as controversial, but

it's really not. This is simply breastfeeding awareness. As this awareness increases, people are likely to become neutral about the subject.

Know that it's ok to nurse away from home. Some new mothers will retreat back to their car to nurse, or you can find a quiet place in public, like a back room. As you get more comfortable with nursing, you may be willing to nurse in an open public place, and this is perfectly fine. You will learn how to cover just enough so that most people will have no idea that you are even breastfeeding!

You are never required to nurse in public, although it is convenient if you are comfortable with it. The first few times may seem uncomfortable, but that will likely go away when you have a hungry baby. And know in the United States (all 50 U.S. states) it is legal to breastfeed in public. Each country has their own rules. Most people will have no problem seeing a little exposure when a baby is breastfeeding. C'est Naturelle!

<u>How long to breastfeed?</u>
How long you breastfeed will be completely up to you, or your baby. It is recommended by the AAP to breastfeed exclusively for 6 months, and after to continue breastfeeding while supplementing other foods until the age of 2, before weaning. Some women will wean before 2 years, and some will nurse past 2 years.

Breastfeeding seems to be more socially acceptable in breastfeeding a baby, but not as much for a toddler. Don't be concerned with what others think if you choose to breastfeed past the age of walking. Because toddlers nurse less frequently than infants, this will be less of a problem than imagined.

Toddlers are busy and will nurse less but more efficiently, using less of your time. Sometimes toddlers will nurse more for snuggles or for bedtime. It is much easier to wean a toddler than it is to wean an infant, so it may just be easier to continue in breastfeeding.
You never know when the last time you will breastfeed. You will look down to see your baby growing up, wondering where the time has gone, but you will carry with you all the memories of your time in breastfeeding. This is the most precious gift you can have.

Perfumes
This one may seem crazy, but one of the most accentuated senses of a newborn is smell. If a baby's sense of smell helps guide them to the breast for survival, it makes sense that a newborn may be sensitive to perfumes.

Babies are more sensitive, so natural products will simply be better than perfumed brands. Try to limit perfumes in baby soaps, lotions, wipes, and laundry detergents. Instead, opt for unscented. Some natural scents are good, but avoid using essential oils due to their concentrated properties. Limit contact with people who wear a lot of perfumes as well.

Natural food grade oils are a good option for moisturizing a baby, or for massage. Olive oil & coconut oil are both edible, and are much better if ingested than mineral oil products. You can do a sample test on the baby before a full application, to test for allergies.

<u>Be Kind</u>
Try not to judge yourself or others in their level of success in breastfeeding. Believe in yourself and your choices. Support breastfeeding by supporting other mothers without judgment. Every mother at one time or another will question their choices and doubt their success. You can only try and do your best at breastfeeding, and the same goes for parenting.

<u>Embrace Love</u>
The early days of becoming new parents can be a lot to adjust to. Each age brings us through new experiences, from checking to see if a newborn is breathing, to placing a toddler back in

bed. Change is inevitable, and that little baby who wakes up through the night will one day become a teenager who wants to lock you out of their room! Embrace all stages of your child, and try to enjoy each day of parenting as you experience it.

Most of all, always Love Your Children. Don't be afraid to show your affection for your children.

C. Contraindications to breastfeeding

This section is not intended to replace medical advice. Always seek professional medical advice when dealing with a medical issue.

HIV/ Radioactive meds/ recreational drugs
There are only a handful of reasons why a woman should not attempt to breastfeed.
If you are **HIV** positive, you should not breastfeed. HIV can pass into breastmilk.
If you are on **Radioactive medicine** or therapy, you should not breastfeed. The risk of transferring radioactive medicine is dangerous to a baby. If you use **recreational drugs,** including cocaine, heroin, or marijuana, you should not breastfeed. Not only can recreational drugs be passed into breastmilk, but it can affect your ability to care for your child, putting children in danger. Always choose **not** to do drugs while raising children. Reach out for help if drugs are a problem.

Prescription Meds

Discuss any and all Prescription Medications & Over-The-Counter Supplements/Medications with your doctor/pediatrician/breastfeeding specialist before starting breastfeeding. Some medications will be
allowed while breastfeeding, and others will not. Never assume a medication is safe to use while breastfeeding; always ask.

Genetic disorder

Mother's milk is the best milk for a baby, but there is always an exception to the rule. The exception here is a rare condition called **galactosemia**. Galactosemia is where the baby doesn't produce an enzyme to digest galactose, which is a simple sugar found in breast milk. If a baby drinks the breast milk and has galactosemia, this will result in a build-up in galactose.

Galactose is not to be confused with lactose, and this condition is not the same as lactose intolerant. If a mother continues to breastfeed a baby with galactosemia, this will cause malabsorption issues in the infant. Galactosemia can cause a serious condition of failure to thrive and possibly cause complications such as brain damage, cataracts, organ failure or death.

But don't worry, this should be ruled out with your pediatrician. Malabsorption will show in symptoms of vomiting, diarrhea and hepatic issues, which should be caught early by the pediatrician at the *well child care visits*.

Hypoplastic breasts
During pregnancy, breasts are growing and developing the milk ducts for breastfeeding. The exception to the rule is when a congenital condition exists when the breasts don't fully develop.

This condition is otherwise known as insufficient glandular tissue, or IGT. This lack of development is called hypoplastic breasts which may result in a lack of breast milk production. Another name for this condition is tubular breasts due to the elongated breast shape, and bulbous areola. Fully developed breasts are round and fuller. Sometimes only one breast doesn't fully develop, looking much smaller than the other breast.

Hypoplastic breasts can be diagnosed by a physician, but the level of milk production won't be known until you attempt to breastfeed. If the breasts are truly tubular, the likelihood for need of supplementation is high.

Diabetes
It is safe and healthy to breastfeed with diabetes, however there may be a few things to note.

Diabetes may result in blood sugar fluctuations, so frequent monitoring and control of blood sugar is highly recommended, especially during pregnancy and postpartum. The stress from delivery and caring for a baby can be a challenge on the body of any mother, but especially on one that is diabetic. Be sure to be in consultation with your physician during and after pregnancy.

The milk supply for a mother with diabetes may delay the milk from coming in. Although colostrum is available, mature milk for a first time mother typically comes in between day 3 & 4, but for a mother who is diabetic, the transitional milk may not come in until day 5 or 6 days. This delay may require supplementation of formula for the baby in the beginning. The continuation of frequent breastfeeding for stimulation to the mammary glands is important. Lactation specialists should be consulted with a breastfeeding mother with diabetes.

Breastfeeding with diabetes can actually help lower your blood sugar, but be sure it doesn't get too low. Always eat healthy and frequent meals, helping to maintain control over your blood sugar while breastfeeding. Be sure your support is aware of signs of hypoglycemia in the first weeks postpartum.

<u>Other Endocrine issues</u>
Some endocrine issues can affect the production of milk. The endocrine system is a complex system that basically centers around the pituitary; the master gland.

Reproduction and Breastfeeding rely on hormones from this system. The pituitary gland secretes specific hormones like prolactin, to help produce milk. The pituitary also helps the thyroid release thyroid hormones.

Oxytocin is produced in the hypothalamus but is stored and released in the posterior pituitary. It is a complex system of hormones and any issues in the endocrine system can affect the body in many ways. Some endocrine issues, such as thyroid disease, will cause breastfeeding problems.

<u>Breast augmentation and Breastfeeding</u>
Will you be able to breastfeed with implants?
Breast augmentation typically involves implanting a shell into the breast tissue to help make the breast appear larger. Each woman has a unique situation of how much the breast tissue has been altered, and the placement of that implant. It comes down to how much the augmentation alters the tissues, nerves or ductwork, which directly affects the milk production or flow. If there is scarring, damage to the milk ducts, or removal of glandular tissue, there may be some issues in delivering breast milk.

Not all breast alterations will keep you from nursing. Learn the proper techniques to breastfeed and give it a try. It's a good idea to consult with a breastfeeding specialist who is educated in alterations. Close monitoring of baby weight gain is necessary for all breastfeeding mothers, especially in those who have potential issues in producing breast milk from augmentation.

VI. Breastfeeding Reference Terms

Antepartum

Before the birth of a child.

Areola & Montgomery glands

The areola is the darkened skin located around the **Nipple** of the breast. The areola features the Montgomery glands, a sebaceous gland that secretes an oil. This oil is secreted to lubricate and protect the delicate breast area, and also to emit an odor which is familiar to the newborn. It is believed to smell similar to the amniotic fluid after birth, which attracts babies to this area. This is an instinctive draw toward the breast after birth, helping lead the newborn to breastfeed.

The number of Montgomery glands per areola can vary. They may grow larger during pregnancy, and the appearance of them may vary woman to woman. But their main purpose is to emit an oily substance.

Caring for the areola and nipples should be simple water over the breasts. You don't need soap, which can be drying to your breast. If you have discharge that dries and needs to be cleansed off, you can use a natural oil (olive or almond) to wipe off the area; pat dry.

Baby age clarifications

<u>Newborn</u> –refers to the first 28 days

<u>Infant</u> –from birth to one year (12 months)

<u>Preterm Infant or Preemie</u> –infant born before 37 weeks

<u>Full Term Infant</u> –born after 37 weeks

<u>Toddler</u> –from 12 months to 36 months (1-3 years)

<u>Baby</u> –an infant or young toddler

<u>Preschoolers</u> –3 or 4 years

<u>School-aged</u> –5 or 6 years

Baby Bites/Teething
Do you automatically wean your baby when he/she bites you? No.
Your baby will typically start teething around 4 or 5 months, with the eruption of the first set of baby's bottom teeth. When a tooth breaks through for a baby, the most natural thing is to explore where to use it. The place often tested is the breast during a nursing session! Ouch! But don't take it personal, your baby isn't intentionally trying to hurt you. You are their most important person!

Typically when a baby bites, it is at the end of a feeding session after the baby has filled his/her belly. In order to bite, the baby stops nursing and pulls the tongue back off the nipple to reveal the tooth. The baby can't nurse and bite at the same time.

If your initial reaction is to scream, this will be quite an unpleasant surprise to your baby! The next time he/she bites during a nursing session, you should carefully remove your breast from the baby's mouth, and *gently* but *firmly* place your finger onto the baby's tooth saying a firm "no". You will see a look of horror in your child's face, as this may be the first reprimanding of its kind! You can resume nursing after a moment. If the child bites again, you cease the nursing session.
If the baby is hungry, this will be a very young lesson that teaches that biting equals no breastmilk. The baby will learn, or go hungry. Babies are smarter than we think! Many mothers around the world nurse babies with a full set of teeth.

But if you are having serious issues, consult with a lactation counselor.

Break the Latch

Breaking the latch is to release the attachment of the nipple from the baby's mouth. This attachment creates a suction to draw out the milk. If you want to disengage the baby from breastfeeding, it is advised not to just pull the breast out of the baby's mouth.

It is better to gently break the suction by popping a clean finger into the side of the baby's mouth, letting a bit of air in and separating the nipple from the baby's mouth.

Breast care

Your breasts don't need to be washed with soap while you are pregnant or nursing. Rinse them off in the shower or bath and pat dry, and let their natural oils remain.

Your breasts house the Montgomery glands within the areolas which secrete a sebaceous gland oil. This secretion is naturally a skin protector and also emits a scent that your baby recognizes. If you use soap, this will wash off the natural oils, making them more susceptible to dryness and cracking.

Breast Size

You do not need big breasts to breastfeed, you can successfully breastfeed with small breasts. If your breasts get sore in the beginning of pregnancy, this indicates the lactogenesis I stage.

This physiological change typically means you will be able to breastfeed. If you have hypoplasia, or damage to your ductwork, you may have difficulty providing adequate milk.

Colostrum

After birth, the breasts initially produce a thick, yellow to orange milk called Colostrum.

Counting Diapers
Counting wet & poopy diapers is a way of evaluating how the baby is doing the first weeks. Wet diapers can detect whether the baby is getting enough fluids, and poopy diapers detect absorption issues. You should keep count of the amount of diapers for the first weeks.

https://www.verywellfamily.com/how-many-wet-diapers-should-my-baby-have-each-day-284176

Dehydration
Dehydration is a serious concern in infants and young children, and can cause death. If a baby has an illness that involves fever, vomiting or diarrhea, the baby's pediatrician should be contacted. Dehydration is technically when a person loses more water than is replenished, along with electrolytes. The rate of dehydration can happen much quicker in infants than in adults.

Engorgement

Engorgement is when the breasts are overfull, with too much supply. Engorgement can lead to blocked milk ducts or mastitis. If your breasts are swollen, you can 1) take a warm shower to relieve some pressure. 2) breastfeed the baby, if the latch is difficult you can 3) try pumping off some milk to soften the breasts and relieve the pressure 4) massage the breast.

Engorgement is prevented with frequent nursings so the milk does not overcollect in the breasts. Breastfeed frequently, every 1 ½ - 2 hours for the first weeks. Once the breasts are engorged, it can cause problems with latch.

*Prevention is key. Limit pacifiers and bottles, and frequently breastfeed.

A blocked milk duct is where one of the ducts isn't emptied properly. Follow the same methods for engorgement. If you see a red streak or red area on your breast, or if it feels feverish, it may be infected.   You will want to contact your pediatrician.

If the breasts are red all over, or feverish, this could be **Mastitis**, which is a serious medical condition that needs immediate medical treatment. See Mastitis.

Exclusively Breastfeeding

Exclusively breastfeeding means mom is only feeding breastmilk with no other liquids or formula supplementation.   Exclusive breastfeeding is recommended for the first 6 months of an infant's life.

Food Sensitivities

Food sensitivities are foods that a mother eats that may create some distress in a breastfeeding baby.   These are not true allergies. A list of common foods linked to distress in babies includes citrus, broccoli, cabbage, chocolate, milk, caffeine, and hot spices & garlic.
You can keep a food journal to determine the culprits, which can be removed from the mother's diet.   These foods can be reintroduced to the mother's diet at a later time, to re-test the sensitivity.

Feed on Demand

Feeding on Demand is to always breastfeed the baby when the baby indicates hunger. This is the recommended method of breastfeeding, which pays special attention to a baby's cues. However, for a newborn, the suggested feedings of 10-12 times a day are recommended to anticipate early hunger cues.   Feeding on demand does not restrict feedings to a limited schedule. Instead, learn your baby's hunger cues and supply a feeding in response to the baby's demand.

Feeding Cues
Feeding cues are the baby's way of indicating hunger. The baby will communicate physically with the mouth; lip-smacking, sucking sounds, fists to mouth, rooting (the reflex if a baby's cheek is touched, the mouth reaches for it) and growing in agitation. The best way to solve this is to nurse.

Growth Spurt
Just when you you've finished a feeding, your baby seems to want to nurse again! This increase in feedings may be growth spurts.
Growth spurts are a time when your baby will grow quickly, with a higher demand for nutrition. Sometimes a growth spurt is recognized due to an increase in feedings. A baby may increase the number of feedings in a type of "cluster" feeds to gain enough nutrition, often before bed time.

Growth spurt ages are unique to each baby, but here are some average ages: 7-10 days, 3-6 weeks, and 4-6 months.

How often to breastfeed?

The Healthy Children's Center for Breastfeeding suggests nursing every 1-2 hours, or *at least* every 3 hours in the daytime, and *at least* every 4 hours at nighttime (even if you need to wake the baby). You should offer the breast between 10-12 times every 24 hours for a newborn baby.
Always consult with your child's pediatrician in reference to recommended feedings.

Illness

If a baby is ill, he/she may increase frequency of nursing, or extend time at breast for comfort. If the baby is ill, nursing is a good thing to continue. An ill baby may also not refuse to nurse, which is a concern because of the possibility of dehydration. Signs of illness may include crabbiness, lethargy, fever, vomiting and diarrhea. Contact your baby's pediatrician anytime an illness is suspected.

Infant cries when nursing

If a baby seems enthusiastic about nursing, but cries and pulls off after trying to nurse, check these:

*check for proper latch/seal for proper milk transfer

*check for audible milk swallows; 2 sucks to 1 swallow (milk availability)

*check for tongue-tie which can cause attachment issues

*rule out illness/ reflux/ gas

A baby shouldn't cry when attempting to nurse. You will want to consult with a lactation specialist if the baby isn't content with nursing.
If a baby nurses happily, but cries when removed from the breast, try continuing to nurse longer, and alternate breasts.

Lactogenesis

Lactogenesis is the production of Milk.
Lactogenesis 1 begins while the mother is pregnant, and begins production of colostrum.

After the delivery of baby and the placenta, Lactogenesis 2 begins, which brings in transitional milk around day 3 postpartum.

Lactogenesis 3 develops only in breastfeeding after around Day 10 postpartum, bringing in the mature milk.

Latch

A latch is the attachment of the baby's mouth over the areola and nipple, which creates a suction to draw out the milk. A Proper latch is when the baby's mouth is flanged open and closed over the mother's nipple and areola, creating a seal. This seal allows for an efficient transfer of milk to flow and be swallowed without air.

Mastitis

Mastitis is a serious breast infection where the breast becomes inflamed and infected. It is often caused from engorgement, a blocked milk duct, or not emptying the breast completely. Other causes may be attachment issues such as improper seal, or even caused by an opportune bacteria through a cracked nipple.

If you have symptoms of a red, feverish breast, and are running a temperature with fatigue, you will need to contact your physician immediately. Mastitis occurs more often in early breastfeeding.

Mature Milk

Mature milk comes in after around day 10. This milk is high in protein and has adequate fat, especially toward the end of a feed, hindmilk. It is more watery than transitional milk and colostrum, and may look bluish in color.

Milk Letdown

The milk flow to the breast is called the letdown. Oxytocin causes an involuntary reflex which releases milk, allowing it to flow into the breasts.
The breasts feel heavy and full when the milk *lets down* each time you breastfeed. The letdown in the beginning may feel a bit uncomfortable, creating a warm and tingly or stingy sensation, but should ease up a few months into breastfeeding.
If the letdown is forceful, it can be difficult for some babies to keep up, resulting in coughing. Release the latch and wait until baby relaxes and is ready to try again.

Milk Supply

Colostrum is available after delivery, until transitional milk is produced around day 3.
Transitional milk begins filling the breast after 3-5.

<u>Mature</u> milk comes in around day 10, but only with consistent breastfeeding. You build up your milk supply from the demand the baby has while suckling at the breast.

A good milk supply is one that satisfies the baby's demands. After baby has a full feeding, the baby will typically show satiety through relaxation in his/her body.

One of the misconceptions many new mothers have is to assume her milk supply isn't adequate. Although this may be true *before* the transitional milk comes in, a mature milk supply is in response to the frequency of feedings. Offer the breast 10-12 times a day, and complete the feedings to the baby's needs. A typical feeding will last until the baby is no longer interested, roughly between 20-40 minutes.

If in the beginning, you will question your milk supply because it seems like you are always breastfeeding, this is normal! It is challenging in the beginning because it seems the baby only wants to nurse, but this will ease up in a few months.

After your transitional milk comes in (by day 5) you should see drips of milk off the baby's mouth or your breast. You should hear audible swallows for every 1-2 sucks. The baby should seem satisfied at the end of a feed.

Mother Pacifier

A nursing baby is best comforted by the mom's warmth, love and milk. Nursing is the most comfortable place in the world for a newborn! But at times, mom will feel like a pacifier. Very young babies like to fall asleep at the breast, and be held for long times. Just know babies *love* nursing time!

Be patient! Try to anticipate feedings and enjoy this time. If you want a more efficient session, you can try to keep the baby more alert by shifting, or lightly tapping their bottom when they begin to drift off. You can end the session when the baby is no longer actively nursing. If the baby doesn't naturally pop off, you can gently *Break the Latch* and move the baby to a safe sleeping place.

Enjoy your early breastfeeding time. As the baby grows older, they become more efficient eaters and more independent.

Nipple Shields

Nipple shields are thin plastic devices, used to cover part of the breast and nipple, to help improve a latch by everting the nipple a bit. Be cautious in believing you need a supplemental product in order to breastfeed, as this is often the trap where women are made to feel inadequate at breastfeeding. It seems nipple shields have a bad reputation of being handed out more frequently than they are needed.

If the latch is challenging in the beginning, try to solve the problem naturally. A specialist can evaluate the baby's mouth, and identify mother's type of nipple.   Sometimes a difficult latch can be due to inverted nipples or tongue-tie. Working through it may help to prevent becoming reliant on nipple shields.

Nipple shields may restrict the amount of milk flow and they make breastfeeding more complex and expensive.   If you feel you can only breastfeed with nipple shields, you will need to work with a lactation specialist to be sure the infant is receiving enough milk.

Nipple types
You don't need perfect breasts to breastfeed. In fact, every woman has unique breasts, just like a fingerprint. But when it comes to breastfeeding, the size of the breast has little impact, but occasionally the type of nipple does. The milk flows from the ductwork through the nipple to deliver milk to the baby. Nipples need to evert out to deliver milk

You should identify your nipple type: There are 3 general types of nipples; Normal, Flat & Inverted.

Normal, or average nipples, are healthy nipples that evert outward, beyond the areola. This is the most common type and the best anatomical nipple for breastfeeding. The nipple usually has no issues delivering milk.

Flat nipples are healthy nipples that lie flat when warm. Many of these flat nipples will evert out when stimulated or cold. You can do a simple pinch test to stimulate the nipple to evert them. You can also try a breast pump for suction, to see if the nipples will stand out. If they do, they will be fine for nursing.

Inverted nipples are also healthy nipples, but can present a problem when it comes to breastfeeding. Inverted nipples may block that flow from the ductwork, making it difficult to deliver milk. You can test your nipples in the manner you test the flat nipples. If they evert outward, you may be able to breastfeed. The true test to breastfeeding is with the baby. Just know if you have inverted nipples and wish to breastfeed, you can try, but it may be best to work with a lactation specialist in the beginning.

Postpartum
After the birth of the child.

Proper Latch
(see latch)

Poop color and consistency of an Infant
The baby's first feces is called meconium, and is dark green and almost black. It will turn a brighter green, and then yellow before day 5 (if breastfeeding).

Exclusively breastfed poop will be yellow and seedy, which represents breastmilk passing through digestive juices and bile. Breastfed poop will be thinner and more frequent than formula fed poop. Expect 5-6 poops a day after 1 week. This number can be variable and should be discussed at the *well child care visits*.

Formula fed poop will be pasty and light brown, more odorous and less frequent than breastfed poops.

Poop that is very malodorous, has mucous or blood in it, or is chalky white can indicate a health issue or malabsorption. This should be brought up to the baby's pediatrician.

Satiety
Satiety is the state of satisfaction after a feed. If the baby has adequately transferred and swallowed adequate milk, there will be satisfaction on the baby's face, with the baby's arms dropping off to the side in relaxation.

Supply & Demand
The law of supply and demand in breastfeeding means the baby demands (suckles at the breast) the supply (amount of breastmilk). When the baby nurses longer, the milk supply increases.

Transitional Milk

Transitional milk comes it around day 3-5. This milk is full of protein and fat and has a creamy appearance. When transitional milk comes in your breasts will feel very full.

Thriving

Thriving means to prosper, or flourish. In baby terms it basically means the baby is absorbing the proper nutrition and is growing adequately.

Weight Gain

An indicator of thriving is weight gain. Weight checks are done to ensure proper weight gain in an infant.

Yeast Infection of the breast

If you have a yeast infection of the breast, or your baby has thrush, these need to be treated by a medical doctor.

Thrush is a type of fungal infection caused by an overgrowth of yeast, which can pass from breast to baby's mouth. The symptoms for the breast will include a pink or shiny nipple that can be painful during a nursing. Symptoms from the baby may include white patches on the cheeks or tongue, which can cause pain while nursing.

Thrush is an infection that can contaminate surfaces. Be sure to sterilize bottles and devices that touch the breast or baby's mouth while treating a thrush infection.

V. The Author's Experience in Breastfeeding

As a child, I remember my mother breastfeed my two younger brothers. I always knew I would breastfeed my babies too.

When I had my first child, I had the support from my husband, my mother, and mother-in-law. I had a hospital program checking up on me. They gave me the confidence I needed to follow through in breastfeeding. Of course I ran into problems, but my hospital support program really helped me solve issues early on, which kept me breastfeeding. Today I realize that support and help in desperate times is key to successful breastfeeding mothers.

When I began breastfeeding my first baby, my milk seemed to take forever to come in. But when it finally did, her milky pursed lips told us she'd gotten a belly full! I will never forget that image! She went on to develop a lip blister from nursing, and I developed cracked, bleeding nipples. This may've been the result of a poor latch. I remember her position feeling awkward in the beginning, and she would often cough from the milk flow. But the latch and position improved, and her ability to nurse was stronger and the problems went away, only left with the sweet baby time.

I felt confident in breastfeeding, and would nurse at friend's homes, and even in public places.
If I was travelling, I'd nurse in the car, I even breastfed in the church pew! I grew confident and felt comfortable feeding when my baby was hungry. When she was about 5 months of age, I recognized she had a signal to nurse –a little fake cough! It was her cute little way to communicate to me that she was hungry! Staring straight up at me, I realized this wonderful connection we shared. I surpassed my breastfeeding goal of 6 months and nursed until 15 months.

I nursed my 2nd child for 11 months, just shy of a year. Both children seemed to wean themselves. My third child wanted to continue nursing past 2, but the feedings were only 1-2 times a day after a year.

Breastfeeding was the most precious time I spent with each of my children, and yet it served a healthy purpose. When my last child was one, I decided to volunteer for the same hospital program that helped me, helping other new moms.

Today, I am dedicated to educating others on breastfeeding.

About the Author

Gina Michelle is a Certified Lactation Counselor and Master's graduate, with 15 years' experience as an educator. She is married with 3 beautiful children she breastfed.   She volunteered 6 ½ years for a hospital program helping new mothers in breastfeeding and parenting.

M.A., CLC